The Legacy of Avoidance

A Journal for Those Learning to Stay When Love Feels Unsafe

by **Katerina Markadakis**

Epigraph

*"Healing begins when we stop running from what still hurts
and learn to sit beside it instead."*

— K.M.

Publisher: Harbor Point Press — Seaford, New York

The Legacy Series Note

The Legacy Series began as stories about silence — how we leave, return, and learn to love again.

Through the four novels — Legacy of Silence, Legacy of Longing, Legacy of Healing, and Legacy of Becoming — we meet characters who carry grief, distance, and the quiet wish to be understood.

The companion works — The Legacy of Avoidance and The Legacy of Letting Go, each with its own guided journal — were created for the reader who saw themselves inside those pages.

Together, these books hold one intention: to remind us that love and healing are never separate stories.

They are simply different ways of coming home.

"From Page to Healing"

These journals were never meant to be read quickly.

They are places to breathe, to pause, to notice what still feels tender.

Let the words meet you gently.

Some pages may echo your past; others may point toward what's next.

You don't need to finish every prompt — you only need to begin.

The work of healing isn't about doing it right.

It's about staying long enough to listen.

Preface

When I started writing about avoidance, I was trying to understand why some people run from love.

What I learned is that most of us aren't running from others — we're running from the feeling of being unworthy of staying.

If you've ever felt safer in distance than in closeness, this journal is for you.

It's a space to meet the part of you that still hides when things feel too real.

Move slowly.

There's no rush here.

Each reflection is an open door — step through only when you're ready.

Healing has its own rhythm, and it will always wait for you.

Dedication

For the ones learning that safety can exist inside connection — may these pages hold you while you practice staying.

AUTHOR'S NOTE

Dear Reader,

You began this journal not to fix yourself,
but to understand yourself,
to meet the parts of you that once hid behind independence
and composure.

Avoidance is not a flaw;
it is a language your heart learned to survive.
But now,
you are learning a new language, one of presence,
vulnerability, and repair.

You have done something sacred:
you turned toward what once terrified you.
You stayed.
And in doing so,
you have rewritten the legacy.

May these pages remind you, always,
that awareness is not punishment, it is freedom;
that connection is not danger, it is healing;
that love is not a performance, it is practice.

And that you, too,
are capable of staying.

With gentleness and reverence,
Katerina Markadakis

★ ★ ★

Purpose

Before there was distance, there was fear.
Before there was silence, there was longing.
Before there was withdrawal, there was a child who learned
that love could hurt.

This journal is not an accusation.
It is an invitation to understand the legacy that lives beneath
avoidance.
To look at the patterns you built not as flaws, but as
protections that have simply outlived their purpose.

It is for the ones who keep their hearts behind walls.
For those who have mastered detachment, self-reliance, and
control, yet still feel the quiet ache of loneliness beneath it all.

This book is your mirror and your mercy.
It will not shame you for how you've survived,
but it will ask you to see how your survival has also kept you
from connection.

It is time to unlearn the safety of distance,
and remember the courage of presence.

You cannot rewrite what shaped you,
but you can choose what you pass on.
You can end the legacy of avoidance with awareness, honesty,
and love.

★ ★ ★

Opening: Preface – For the Ones Who Pull Away

Before you began to leave,
you learned to disappear.

Not all at once, but quietly,
in the pauses between conversations,
in the way you folded your feelings into silence,
in the moments you convinced yourself
you were safer alone.

You became an expert at composure,
a master of self-control.
You learned that needing less made you unbreakable,
that being untouched meant being untouchable.

But in protecting yourself from pain,
you also walled yourself off from love.

You tell yourself you prefer peace,
but what you really mean is predictability —
no surprises, no rejection, no risk.
Still, somewhere deep down,
you crave to be known,
to be met,
to be chosen,
without having to hide.

This journal is for that part of you,
the one that still hopes closeness could one day feel like
safety,
that vulnerability might not always mean loss.

You will not be asked to confess or apologize.
You will be asked to notice.
To pause before the exit.
To listen to the voice that says stay,
even when every instinct says run.

You have spent years learning to protect yourself from
love.
Now it is time to learn how to receive it.

This is your beginning,
not of perfection,
but of presence.

Because the legacy ends
the moment you choose to stay.

Katerina Markadakis

* * *

Table of Contents

PART I – THE INHERITANCE OF ABSENCE

Where Distance First Learned Your Name

Before you built walls,
you built silence.
You learned to hold your breath when love walked into the
room,
to shrink your needs into something small enough not to be
noticed.

Avoidance is not born from cruelty.
It is born from absence,
from the quiet lessons taught in moments no one remembers:
a parent too busy to notice,
a hug that never came,
an emotion dismissed before it could form a name.

You learned that closeness could be unpredictable,
that love could change its temperature without warning.
And so, you made a quiet vow:
"I will not need what can disappear."

This vow became your inheritance,
a legacy passed down not through words,
but through the echo of unmet needs.

* * *

You grew up fluent in withdrawal.
You learned how to soothe yourself,
how to stay busy,
how to appear fine even when something inside you ached
for contact.

You became independent,
so independent that you began to equate solitude with
strength.

But independence without intimacy is only isolation in
disguise.
And the heart, no matter how silent,
still hungers for belonging.

Avoidance is not an absence of love,
it is the fear of being seen in your longing for it.
Because to be seen means to be vulnerable,
and vulnerability once meant danger.

So you stayed hidden,
and the world called it strength.

★ ★ ★

Reflection Prompts

(1) When you think back to your childhood, what did love look like in your home?

_____
_____
_____
_____
_____

(2) What happened when you expressed your needs or emotions?

_____
_____
_____
_____
_____

(3) What silent lessons did you learn about safety, affection, or attention?

_____
_____
_____
_____
_____

(4) When did closeness first begin to feel unsafe for you?

_____

_____

_____

_____

_____

★ ★ ★

The Roots of Control

Control is the armor of the avoidant heart.
You keep your world neat, predictable,
free from emotional mess.
You say you value peace,
but often what you value most is control over the unknown.

Because unpredictability once meant pain.
It meant rejection, ridicule, or being invisible.

So now, when someone gets too close,
you retreat into the only safety you know,
distance.

You convince yourself that you're protecting your peace,
but in truth, you're protecting your wounds.

And yet, there's a part of you,
small, quiet, unbroken,
that still wants to be reached.

That part is your beginning.
It's not the part that leaves.
It's the part that longs to stay.

★ ★ ★

(1) What do you notice happens inside you when someone wants to get closer?

_____

_____

_____

_____

_____

(2) How do you protect yourself from feeling too much?

_____

_____

_____

_____

_____

(3) What might it feel like to be fully seen — and still accepted?

_____

_____

_____

_____

_____

★ ★ ★

Affirmation

I honor the parts of me that learned to survive through distance.
I no longer shame the silence that once kept me safe,
but I am learning that safety can also be found in connection.

I am ready to understand the absence that shaped me,
and to choose presence instead.

★ ★ ★

PART II – THE MASK OF INDEPENDENCE

How Strength Became a Disguise for Fear

There's a kind of strength the world applauds,
the one that never asks for help,
never cries,
never needs.

You built that strength like armor.
Every achievement, every wall,
became another layer of proof that you could survive on your own.

You told yourself it was maturity.
You told others it was confidence.
But deep down,
you knew it was defense.

Because independence, for the avoidant heart,
is not always freedom,
it's the safest form of control.

★ ★ ★

In healthy love, independence and intimacy coexist.
But when closeness once meant pain,
independence becomes protection from intimacy itself.

You say you need space,
but what you really mean is safety.
You say you're busy,
but what you really mean is **you're** afraid.
Afraid that if you are known too deeply,
you will be needed too much.

Avoidance whispers,
"If I keep enough distance, I can't be hurt."
But distance doesn't protect you, it starves you.
It turns solitude into survival.

★ ★ ★

Your nervous system remembers what your mind has
rationalized.
Every time love approached and then withdrew,
your body learned to brace itself.

Now, closeness activates the same alarm.
Your heart speeds up.
Your chest tightens.
You interpret connection as a threat.

So you pull away,
not because you don't care,
but because your body has mistaken love for danger.

This is the paradox of avoidance:
you long for safety,
but the very thing that can heal you, connection,
feels unsafe.

Healing begins when you notice the moment before you
retreat
and choose to stay with yourself instead.

★ ★ ★

Reflection Prompts

(1) When someone offers care or affection,
what happens in your body?

_____

_____

_____

_____

_____

(2) How do you maintain control in relationships,
emotionally, mentally, or physically?

_____

_____

_____

_____

_____

(3) What would happen if you let someone see you struggle
instead of hiding behind strength?

_____

_____

_____

_____

_____

(4) In what moments do you confuse "peace" with "avoidance"?

_____

_____

_____

_____

_____

★ ★ ★

The Myth of Self-Sufficiency

You were praised for being strong,
for needing nothing.
But strength without softness becomes a cage.

Real strength is not the refusal to depend,
it's the courage to trust.

Dependence is not weakness.
It's the shared heartbeat of connection.
It's saying,
"I can stand alone,
but I choose not to always have to."

You were never meant to heal in isolation.
You were meant to be met.

★ ★ ★

(1) What would it mean for you to ask for help without shame?

_____

_____

_____

_____

_____

(2) What kind of love feels both safe and free to you?

_____

_____

_____

_____

_____

(3) Where could you allow softness to replace control?

_____

_____

_____

_____

_____

★ ★ ★

Affirmation

I no longer confuse control with peace.
I am learning that vulnerability is not weakness,
but a quiet kind of courage.

I am safe to need,
safe to ask,
safe to stay.

I release the mask of independence
and let authenticity become my strength.

★ ★ ★

PART III – THE MIRROR OF LOVE

Seeing What Your Distance Has Created

You believed your silence protected both of you.
You thought retreat was mercy,
that stepping back spared them pain.

But distance does not disappear quietly.
It echoes.
It lingers.
It leaves someone waiting in a room full of questions.

They learned to measure your love
not by words,
but by the absence of them.

You didn't mean to teach them that love must be earned,
but every unanswered message,
every half-smile,
every "I'm fine"
became its own kind of lesson.

And now, for the first time,
you're being asked to see what they saw,
not to punish yourself,
but to understand the impact of your absence.

Because healing avoidance begins
when you finally turn around and face what your distance left
behind.

★ ★ ★

To love an avoidant is to love someone through a fog.
To reach, and reach again,
only to touch air.

They learned to lower their voice,
to need less,
to tiptoe around your moods
like emotional landmines.

You didn't ask them to do that,
but they did,
because they loved you,
and they mistook your withdrawal for fragility.

They told themselves,
"If I just love gently enough, he'll stay."
And you told yourself,
"If I just stay calm enough, it won't hurt."

Both of you disappeared,
one into over-giving,
the other into silence.

★ ★ ★

The Compassion of Awareness

It takes courage to admit this:
You didn't avoid love because you didn't care.
You avoided love because you cared too much
and didn't know how to stay without losing yourself.

Avoidance isn't cruelty, it's fear in disguise.
Fear that if you let someone all the way in,
you'll be consumed.
Fear that if you open your heart,
you'll be left exposed again.

But every time you retreat,
you create the very emptiness you fear.
Every time you leave before being left,
you teach yourself that connection cannot last.

Awareness is the beginning of repair.
It is not an apology yet,
it is the pause before one.
It is the breath that says,
"I see what I couldn't before."

* * *

(1) What do you imagine it felt like to love you when you were distant?

_____

_____

_____

_____

_____

(2) What patterns do you notice in the way you withdraw from others?

_____

_____

_____

_____

_____

(3) When you picture the person you pulled away from, what emotion rises in you first — guilt, grief, fear, or tenderness?

_____

_____

_____

_____

_____

20 | P a g e

(4) What would it look like to stay open long enough to witness their pain, without collapsing into shame?

_____

_____

_____

_____

_____

* * *

The First Glimpse of Empathy

Empathy is not self-blame.
It's the willingness to see from both sides.

To know that your fear of closeness hurt someone else's fear
of abandonment.
That your silence spoke the same language as their pleading,
both of you desperate to feel safe.

The heart learns empathy when it allows truth to soften it.
Not in guilt,
but in grace.

★ ★ ★

(1) Think of a time you left emotionally before you left physically.
What were you protecting in that moment?

_____

_____

_____

_____

_____

 (2) What would you want to say now to the person who waited for you to return?

_____

_____

_____

_____

_____

(3) How might your relationships change if you chose presence instead of protection?

_____

_____

_____

_____

_____

★ ★ ★

Affirmation

I am learning to see beyond my fear.
I honor the truth that love requires both hearts to stay present.

I am no longer ashamed of my distance,
I am becoming aware of it.

Awareness is my first act of love.
Empathy is my beginning of change.

★ ★ ★

PART IV – THE NERVOUS SYSTEM OF CLOSENESS

Teaching the Body That Love Can Be Safe

Before your mind ever decided to pull away,
your body learned to brace.

Every cell remembers:
the sound of raised voices,
the absence of comfort,
the cold space where warmth should have been.

Your nervous system wrote its own language long before
words:
When closeness comes, tighten. When love approaches,
retreat.

This is not your fault.
It is your body's oldest wisdom,
a survival story written in muscle and breath.

But now, safety no longer means escape.
Safety means staying.
And staying begins in the body.

★ ★ ★

When someone reaches for you, emotionally or physically,
your body scans for danger faster than your thoughts can
explain it.

Your heart may race.
Your chest may feel heavy.
Your mind goes blank or distracted.
You crave space.

That's not you being cold;
that's your nervous system entering protection mode.
What once saved you, distance,
now keeps you from the love you long for.

Avoidance is not just emotional;
it is physiological.

But what was learned can be unlearned.
The body can learn new stories.
Safety can be rewritten through gentleness and repetition.

★ ★ ★

Re-Teaching the Body Safety

Closeness does not have to mean chaos.
It can feel steady.
It can feel quiet.
It can feel like breath shared, not stolen.

When you notice yourself pulling away,
pause.
Place your hand on your heart.
Take one slow breath.
Tell your body,
"I'm safe now."

You do not have to force openness.
You only have to stay one breath longer than the fear.

That is how trust is built,
moment by moment,
breath by breath.

★ ★ ★

(1) What sensations tell you that you're becoming emotionally flooded or unsafe?

_____

_____

_____

_____

_____

(2) How has your body learned to protect you when you feel too close to someone?

_____

_____

_____

_____

_____

(3) What small practice could remind your body that safety and love can coexist?

_____

_____

_____

_____

_____

(4) Who in your life has ever felt safe to be close to, and why?

_____

_____

_____

_____

_____

* * *

Grounding in the Moment

When you feel yourself drifting away mid-conversation, try this:

- Feel your feet on the floor.
- Notice one sound in the room.
- Notice one color around you.
- Breathe in through your nose for four counts, out through your mouth for six.

You are here.
You are safe.
You do not have to disappear.

★ ★ ★

Healing avoidance is not about tearing down all your walls at once.
It's about opening one window.

Let someone's care stay for a few seconds longer.
Let their hand rest on yours before you pull away.
Let their question, "How are you, really?", land fully before you deflect it.

Notice what happens in your chest.
Breathe.
Stay.

This is the slow, sacred work of retraining your nervous system:
to believe that connection can be soft,
and presence can be safe.

★ ★ ★

Your Reflection Space

(1) What does "safety" in love mean to you now?

_____

_____

_____

_____

(2) Where in your body do you feel the most tension when you try to stay present?

_____

_____

_____

_____

(3) What could you whisper to yourself in those moments to remind your body that you are safe?

_____

_____

_____

_____

★ ★ ★

Affirmation

My body is learning that love is not danger.

I no longer have to flee to feel free.

I am safe in connection,
safe in closeness,
safe in my own softness.

Each breath I stay is an act of healing.

* * *

PART V – THE RELEARNING OF PRESENCE

Learning to Stay When Love Feels Unfamiliar

You have spent years mastering the art of leaving.
You left in small ways,
by numbing your feelings,
by changing the subject,
by keeping your heart a few steps behind your words.

But presence is not a performance.
It is the quiet courage of staying,
even when your body trembles with memory.

Staying does not mean losing yourself.
It means meeting yourself,
the part of you that wants to love
without retreating into silence.

★ ★ ★

You were not born distant.
You became that way because you needed to survive.
Now, the survival can rest.

Presence is not something you achieve once and keep forever;
it is something you return to again and again.

Each time you notice the impulse to shut down,
the need to "fix," "explain," or "walk away,"
you have a choice:
pause,
breathe,
and stay.

That moment of pause is sacred.
It is the space where love begins again.

★ ★ ★

To stay means to feel without fleeing.
To listen without defending.
To speak without rehearsing.
To be touched without tightening.

Presence is not comfort, it's commitment.
It's the promise you make to yourself:
"I will not leave myself when things get hard."

When you can stay with your own discomfort,
you can stay with someone else's too.

That is intimacy,
not merging,
but meeting.

★ ★ ★

(1) What does "staying" look like for you, emotionally, mentally, or physically?

_____

_____

_____

_____

_____

(2) What are your signs that you're starting to withdraw or disconnect?

_____

_____

_____

_____

_____

(3) What gentle reminders help you stay present when you want to retreat?

_____

_____

_____

_____

_____

★ ★ ★

Even the most self-aware hearts still pull away sometimes.
That's okay.

Healing is not about never retreating,
it's about returning faster,
with honesty instead of shame.

You can say,
"I shut down for a moment. I'm trying to stay."
You can admit,
"I need a breath, but I'll come back."

These are small bridges,
and they change everything.

Because repair tells love,
I may disappear, but I will not stay gone.

* * *

The Language of Soft Communication

Avoidant love often speaks in silence,
but healing requires new words,
simple, true, uncluttered:

- "I need a moment to collect my thoughts."
- "I care, even when I go quiet."
- "It's hard for me to stay open right now, but I want to try."
- "Please don't mistake my silence for indifference."

Each of these sentences is a door.
Each one says, "I am still here."

★ ★ ★

(1) What truths about your emotions have you never voiced out loud?

_____

_____

_____

_____

_____

(2) How could you begin to share your inner world, slowly and safely, with someone you trust?

_____

_____

_____

_____

_____

(3) What would it mean for you to be known, not for your calm, but for your honesty?

_____

_____

_____

_____

_____

★ ★ ★

When You Want to Leave

When you feel the urge to run,
remember, leaving doesn't always mean movement.
Sometimes it's zoning out,
shutting down,
turning the warmth in your eyes to glass.

Instead of running,
pause.
Say to yourself,
"This is the part where I usually leave, but I'm learning to
stay."

Presence doesn't mean perfection.
It means choice.
It means love by decision, not by reaction.

* * *

Your Reflection Space

(1) What situations make you want to leave the most quickly?

_____

_____

_____

_____

_____

(2) What would staying look like, just for a little longer, in those moments?

_____

_____

_____

_____

_____

(3) What does love look like when you stay?

_____

_____

_____

_____

_____

★ ★ ★

Affirmation

I am learning the language of presence.

I am safe to stay when love feels close.

I can return after I withdraw.

I can speak instead of disappear.

I am no longer a ghost in my own story,
I am here,
fully,
bravely,
and alive.

★ ★ ★

PART VI – THE LEGACY YOU LEAVE BEHIND

Turning Distance Into Devotion

Every pattern carries a lineage.
The silence you learned was not yours alone,
it came from generations who did not know how to stay.

Somewhere, someone before you
also confused control for safety,
quiet for peace,
distance for strength.

But it ends with you.
Because you are here,
reading these words,
listening to the ache that says,
"There must be another way."

And there is.

★ ★ ★

You Are Not the Wound — You Are the Healer

You may not have chosen the distance you inherited,
but you can choose what you pass on.

You are not defined by your avoidance,
you are defined by your awareness.

Healing is not the absence of fear,
but the choice to love through it,
to stay through it,
to breathe through it.

This is your quiet revolution,
to meet love where you once fled.

★ ★ ★

The New Inheritance

Presence is now your legacy.
Softness, your strength.
Truth, your language.

When you stay,
even for one honest breath longer than you used to,
you change everything.

You model safety for those who never saw it.
You show that love can exist without punishment,
that intimacy can bloom without fear.

You teach by example,
that connection is not a trap,
but a home.

★ ★ ★

Reflection Prompts

(1) What patterns of avoidance or emotional distance were modeled for you growing up?

_____

_____

_____

_____

_____

(2) What patterns do you no longer want to pass on to a partner, a child, or anyone you love?

_____

_____

_____

_____

_____

(3) What new legacy are you building — one based on presence, vulnerability, and love?

_____

_____

_____

_____

_____

(4) How can you honor your past without being bound to it?

_____

_____

_____

_____

_____

* * *

Forgiveness as Freedom

Forgiveness is not a forgetting of what was;
it is the choice to stop living as if the past still owns you.

You can forgive the people who didn't stay,
not to excuse their distance,
but to release the echo of it from your body.

You can forgive yourself, too,
for the years you spent running from love,
for the hearts you kept waiting,
for the silence you mistook for strength.

Because now you know,
you were protecting something sacred,
your longing to feel safe.

And now that safety exists within you,
you no longer need to hide.

* * *

(1) Who or what do you still need to forgive to feel free?

_____

_____

_____

_____

_____

(2) What words of compassion would you offer your younger self, the one who first learned to pull away?

_____

_____

_____

_____

_____

(3) What does peace feel like in your body when you imagine letting go of old patterns?

_____

_____

_____

_____

_____

★ ★ ★

A Blessing for the One Who Stays

May you remember that leaving was once survival,
but staying is now strength.

May you honor the distance that once kept you safe,
while walking boldly toward the warmth that waits for you
now.

May your silence turn to softness,
your control to calm,
your independence to intimacy.

And may you find, at last,
that home was never the place you hid,
it was the heart you finally returned to.

* * *

Final Affirmation

I am no longer the absence I inherited.
I am the presence I am creating.

I forgive where I once withdrew.
I repair what I once avoided.

I choose to stay.
I choose to love.

I am the ending of one legacy
and the beginning of another.

★ ★ ★

Letter to the One Who Comes After

Dear You,

I once thought love meant losing myself,
so I stayed hidden behind walls of calm and control.
But now I know love is not what takes from you;
it is what meets you where you are and asks nothing but
truth.

If you ever find yourself wanting to run,
remember, staying is not weakness.
It is the bravest thing you will ever do.

Because presence is how love heals.
And you, too, are worthy of that healing.

With gentleness,
Me

★ ★ ★

Afterword – A Blessing For The One Who Stays

You have traveled through silence and seen its cost.
You have faced the weight of your absence
and the ache of your return.

You have learned that leaving was never the cure for fear,
only a pause in its echo.

But now,
you know something you didn't before:
love does not demand your perfection;
it only asks for your presence.

Staying does not erase the past,
but it rewrites its rhythm.
It teaches your body that safety can exist in connection,
that your heart can remain open
without losing itself.

You are no longer defined by the distance you created;
you are defined by the moment you turned back.

This is not the end of your story;
it is the beginning of your belonging.

* * *

A Prayer for Reconnection

May you learn to breathe inside love
without fearing the next inhale.

May your voice grow stronger
each time you speak instead of withdraw.

May your silence soften
into listening that heals.

May you offer the love you once withheld,
not out of guilt, but out of grace.

And when closeness feels too bright,
may you remember,
you are built to hold the light.

★ ★ ★

BLESSING FOR THE JOURNEY AHEAD

May the fear that once kept you distant
become the wisdom that keeps you kind.

May your hands learn softness,
your voice learn truth,
your heart learn safety in the company of love.

May you no longer confuse peace with silence
or protection with isolation.

May you feel worthy of being seen,
not for your calm,
not for your control,
but for your humanness.

And when old patterns whisper,
"Leave before you are left,"
may you whisper back,
"I am not leaving. I am learning to stay."

You have broken the inheritance of absence.
You have become the legacy of presence.

★ ★ ★

End of *The Legacy of Avoidance – A Journal for Those Learning to Stay When Love Feels Unsafe*

by **Katerina Markadakis**

About the Author

Katerina Markadakis is the author of The Legacy of Avoidance: For Those Learning to Stay When Love Feels Unsafe and its companion, The Legacy of Avoidance — A Journal for Those Learning to Stay When Love Feels Unsafe.

Through her imprint, Harbor Point Press, she writes both fiction and non-fiction that explore love, loss, and the quiet strength of returning to oneself.

Her Legacy Series — Legacy of Silence, Legacy of Longing, Legacy of Healing, and Legacy of Becoming — reveals how our stories become the mirrors that guide us home.

She is also the author of The Legacy of Letting Go: For Those Healing from Love That Could Not Stay and its companion journal.

Katerina lives in Seaford, New York, where she continues to write and publish under Harbor Point Press, creating books that invite readers to find peace in presence and meaning in the spaces between.

Publisher Imprint Page

Published by Harbor Point Press
Seaford, New York | Est. 2025

ISBN: [To be assigned]

www.ingramcontent.com/pod-product-compliance
Lightning Source LLC
Chambersburg PA
CBHW070646130626
46555CB00006B/2734